BUSY BUZZERS

Bees in Your Backyard

Written by Nancy Loewen
Illustrated by Brandon Reibeling

Backyard Bugs

Thanks to our advisers for their expertise,
research, knowledge, and advice:

Gary A. Dunn, M.S., Director of Education
Young Entomologists' Society
Lansing, Michigan

Susan Kesselring, M.A., Literacy Educator
Rosemount-Apple Valley-Eagan (Minnesota) School District

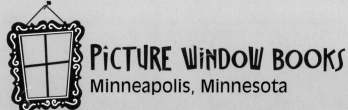

PICTURE WINDOW BOOKS
Minneapolis, Minnesota

Managing Editor: Bob Temple
Creative Director: Terri Foley
Editors: Nadia Higgins, Brenda Haugen
Editorial Adviser: Andrea Cascardi
Copy Editor: Laurie Kahn
Designer: Melissa Voda
Page production: Picture Window Books
The illustrations in this book were prepared digitally.

Picture Window Books
5115 Excelsior Boulevard
Suite 232
Minneapolis, MN 55416
1-877-845-8392
www.picturewindowbooks.com

Printed in the United States of America.

Library of Congress Cataloging-in-Publication Data
Loewen, Nancy, 1964–
Busy buzzers : bees in your backyard / written by Nancy Loewen ; illustrated by Brandon
Reibeling.
p. cm. — (Backyard bugs)
Summary: Describes the physical characteristics, life cycle, and behavior of honeybees.
Includes bibliographical references (p.   ).
ISBN 1-4048-0143-X (hardcover)
1. Bees Juvenile literature. [1. Honeybee. 2. Bees.] I. Reibeling, Brandon, ill. II. Title.
QL565.2 .L64 2003
595.79'9—dc21
                                                                        2003006098

Table of Contents

4

A Flower's Friend

Don't you just love flowers? They're so bright and pretty, and they smell so good. But wait—don't stick your nose too close to that one! There's a honeybee on it. You don't have to be scared, though. It won't sting you as long as you don't bother it.

Why do you think there are so many bees here in the flower garden? It's because flowers aren't just pretty to a bee—they're lunch! Bees drink nectar, which is a sweet liquid found in flowers.

A bee's tongue is a long tube that works like a drinking straw. It can be rolled up or held out straight.

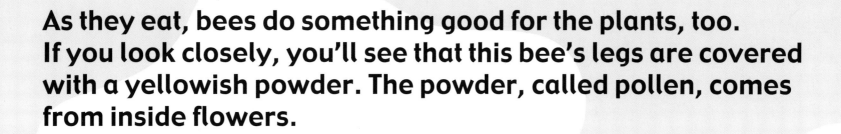

As they eat, bees do something good for the plants, too.
If you look closely, you'll see that this bee's legs are covered
with a yellowish powder. The powder, called pollen, comes
from inside flowers.

As bees fly about, they spread pollen from one flower
to another. That helps the plants make seeds.

Honeybees also collect pollen
and feed it to their young.

Hives and Honey

Look! There's a beehive inside that old tree stump. The bees made the hive out of wax from their bodies. They filled the hive with thousands of tiny rooms called cells.

As many as 50,000 bees could be living inside the hive. All the bees work together as a team, or colony.

There are 20,000 kinds of bees in the world. Not all bees live in colonies.

The main job of a honeybee colony is—you guessed it—
to make honey! The bees' bodies turn nectar into honey.
Then, the bees store the honey in the cells of the hive.
The honey is food for all the bees in the colony.

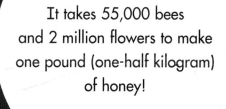

It takes 55,000 bees
and 2 million flowers to make
one pound (one-half kilogram)
of honey!

The Queen Bee

In a beehive, every bee has an important job to do. The queen bee lays the eggs. She doesn't have time to do anything else. In the summer, she lays between 1,200 and 2,000 eggs every day!

Male bees, called drones, mate with the queen as they fly high in the air. After mating, the males die.

There can be only one queen in the colony. Other bees might kill extra queens or kick them out of the hive. Sometimes the queens battle with one another until only one is left.

Busy Bees

The worker bees, which are all female, do everything else. They feed the queen and take care of the young. They look for flowers and bring nectar and pollen back to the hive. They clean the hive and build new cells.

Worker bees fan their wings to keep the hive at just the right temperature. In very hot weather, they bring water to the hive to cool it down.

Dancing Bees

Bees have a great way of talking to one another—by dancing! If a bee finds a lot of tasty flowers, it goes back to the hive and flies in the shape of an 8. This is called a waggle dance. From that dance, the other bees can tell where the flowers are, how far away they are, and even how good they are.

Bees also dance to show that more bees are needed to find flowers or to make nectar into honey.

Summer Sounds

Buzzzzzzz.

Shh. Close your eyes. Do you hear a quiet buzzing sound? Bees buzz like that by making their wings shiver. They're trying to loosen grains of pollen in the flowers.

Doesn't it sound like summer?

Life Cycle of a Honeybee

1. The queen bee lays eggs in some of the cells of the beehive. There can be only one egg in a cell.

2. In three days, the eggs hatch into larvae. The larvae don't have wings, legs, or even eyes. They look like grains of rice with mouths.

3. Worker bees feed the larvae a mixture of pollen and honey called bee bread. A few larvae might be fed "royal jelly" from a young worker bee's head. These larvae become queen bees.

4. The larvae grow and develop jaws. After six days, the larvae spin cocoons. They will become adult bees in 8 to 10 days.

   - Queen bees live the longest, from one to three years.

   - Drones live only a few weeks.

   - Worker bees that hatch in summer live five to six weeks. Those that hatch in the fall, however, live all winter. They huddle together in the hive to stay warm. They eat the honey that other worker bees stored in the hive during the summer.

Fun Facts

- A worker bee's stinger has a little hook at the end. When a worker bee stings an animal, the stinger pulls out of the bee's body as the bee flies away. The worker bee soon dies. Queen bees have smooth stingers, so they can sting over and over. Drones don't have stingers at all.

- Bumblebees make honey, too, but they don't store it the way honeybees do. They live in smaller colonies that die out every autumn, except for the queen. In the spring, the queen starts a new colony.

- During a food-hunting trip, a worker bee visits between 50 and 100 flowers.

- Bees can't fly if it gets too cold. The muscles they use for flying don't work.

- Bees have five eyes. Their two big eyes are good at seeing movement. They also have three small eyes that are good at seeing light. Drones have extra-big eyes so they are sure to see the queen bee as she flies.

Go on a Honey Hunt

People have been eating honey for thousands of years. Many people raise bees to make honey. The flavor and color of honey is affected by the kinds of flowers from which the bees get the nectar. In the United States, you can buy as many as 300 different kinds of honey!

The next time you're at the grocery store, take a close look at the honey section. Read the labels, and see how many different kinds of honey you can find. Take a look in the store for some of the ways people use honey in other foods. (Hint: Look closely at cereal boxes.)

Words to Know

cells – The six-sided rooms in a honeybee's hive are called cells.

colony – A colony is a large group of insects that live and work together as a team.

drone – A drone is a male bee.

mate – Male and female bees mate by joining together special parts of their bodies. After they've mated, the female can lay eggs.

nectar – Nectar is a sweet liquid found in flowers.

pollen – Pollen is a yellowish powder that comes from flowers. Plants need pollen to make seeds and bear fruit.

23

To Learn More

At the Library

Allen, Judy. *Are You a Bee?* New York: Kingfisher, 2001.
Brimner, Larry Dane. *Bees.* New York: Children's Press, 1999.
Gibbons, Gail. *The Honey Makers.* New York: Morrow Junior Books, 1997.
Heinrichs, Ann. *Bees.* Minneapolis: Compass Point Books, 2002.

On the Web

enature.com
http://www.enature.com/guides/select_Insects_and_Spiders.asp
Articles about and photos of almost 300 species of insects and spiders

The National Park Service
http://www1.nature.nps.gov/wv/insects.htm
A guide to finding and studying insects at national parks

University of Kentucky Department of Entomology
http://www.uky.edu/Agriculture/Entomology/ythfacts/entyouth.htm
A kid-friendly site with insect games, jokes, articles, and resources

Fact Hound
Fact Hound offers a safe, fun way to find Web sites related to this book.
All of the sites on Fact Hound have been researched by our staff.
http://www.facthound.com

1. Visit the Fact Hound home page.
2. Enter a search word related to this book, or type in this special code: 140480143X.
3. Click on the FETCH IT button.

Your trusty Fact Hound will fetch the best sites for you!